Animal Helpers:
Wildlife Rehabilitators

by Jennifer Keats Curtis

with Mary Birney,
Victoria Campbell,
Kim Johnson,
Randy Loftus,
Miriam Moyer,
and Kathy Woods

Experts who care for sick, hurt, or orphaned wild animals are called wildlife rehabilitators. They are far more than critter sitters.

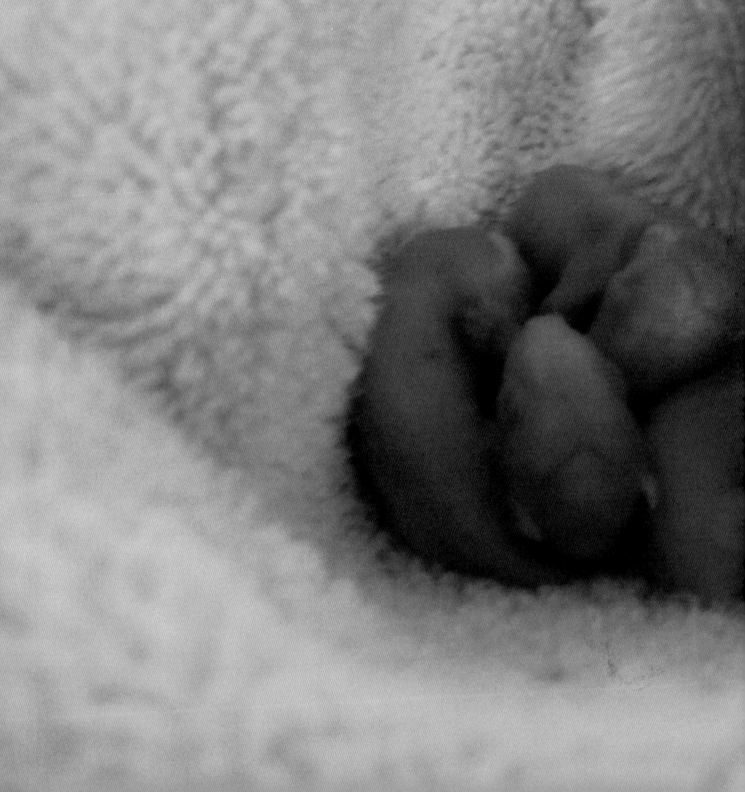

Rehabilitators feed and care for orphaned baby animals, like these baby opossums, until they are old enough to survive on their own.

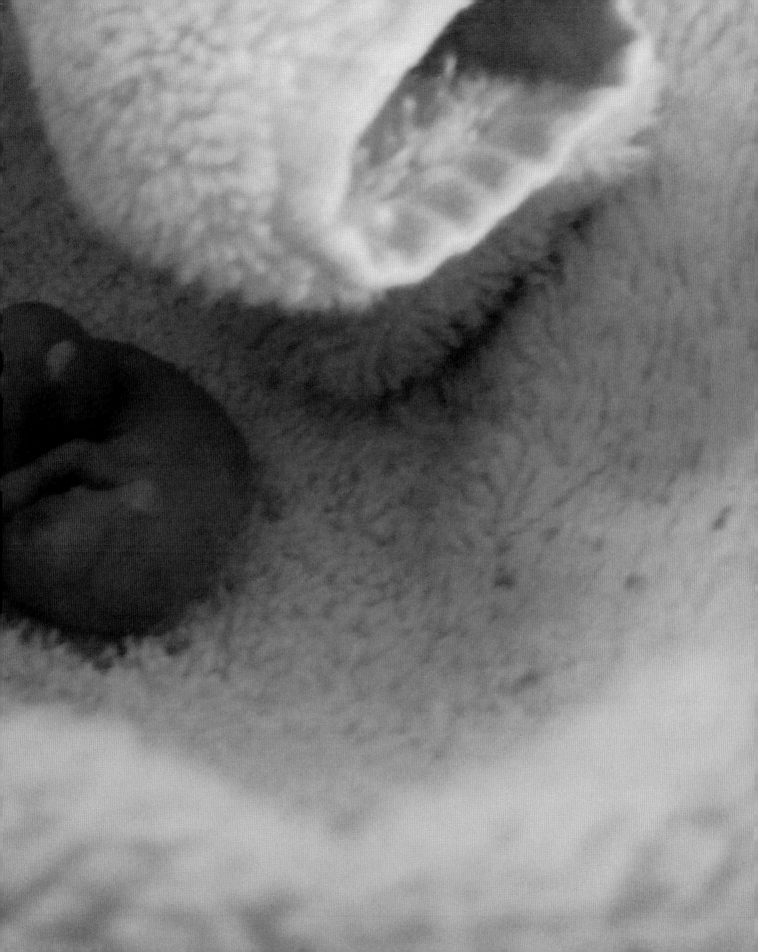

Young mammals, like this raccoon, drink special milk from bottles.

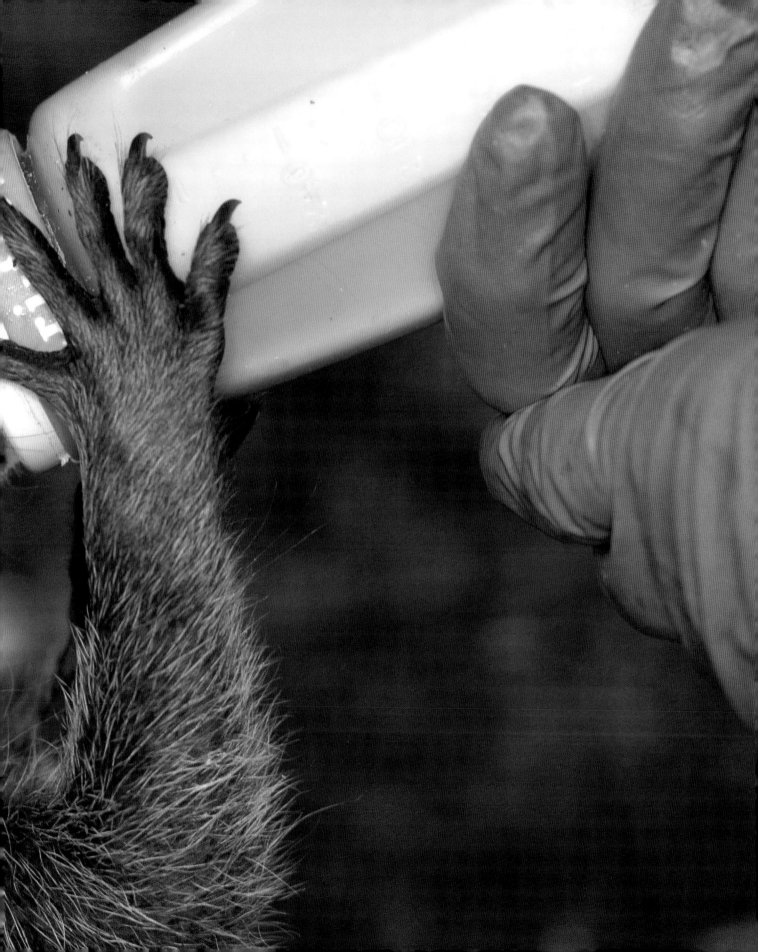

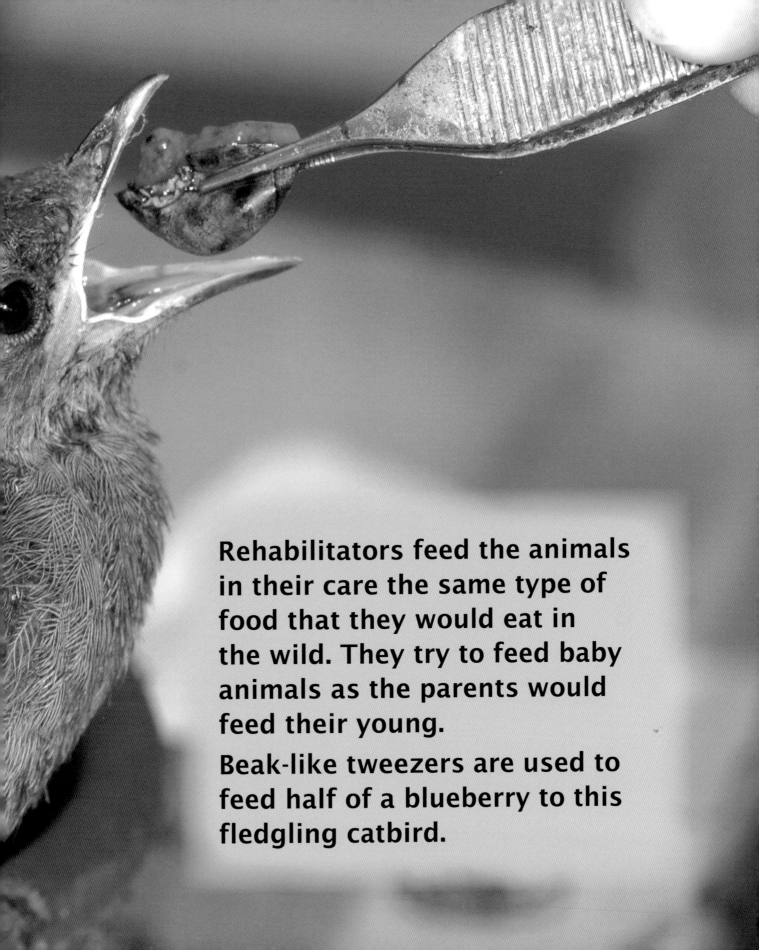

Rehabilitators feed the animals in their care the same type of food that they would eat in the wild. They try to feed baby animals as the parents would feed their young.

Beak-like tweezers are used to feed half of a blueberry to this fledgling catbird.

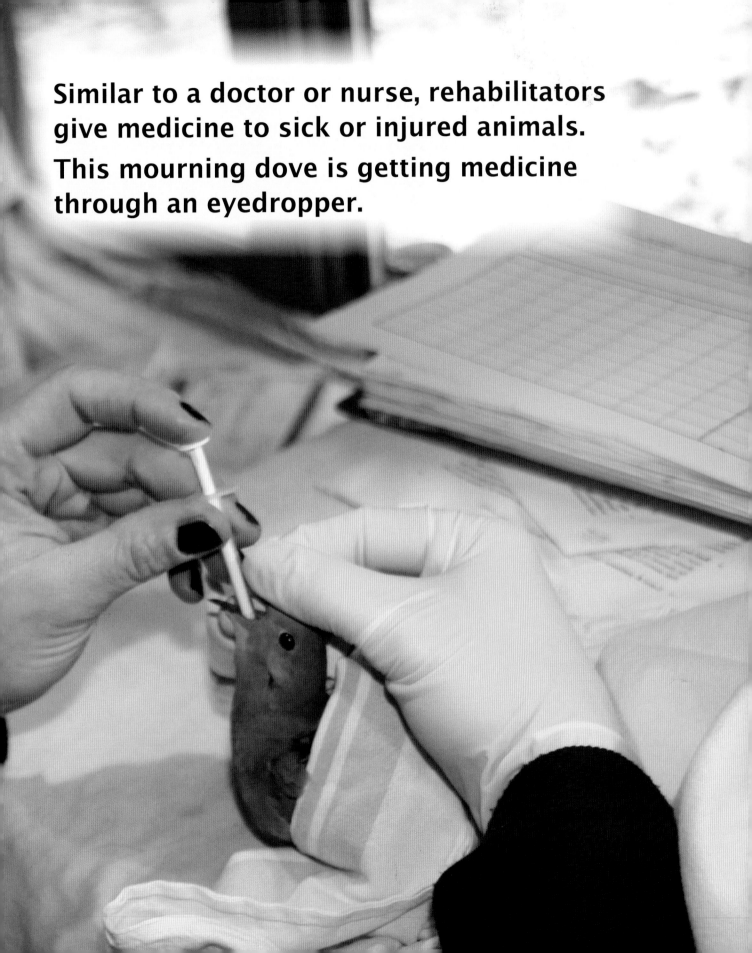

Similar to a doctor or nurse, rehabilitators give medicine to sick or injured animals. This mourning dove is getting medicine through an eyedropper.

Rehabilitators make safe shelters for the animals— a tissue-box home for these opossums . . .

. . . a playpen for
these fawns . . .

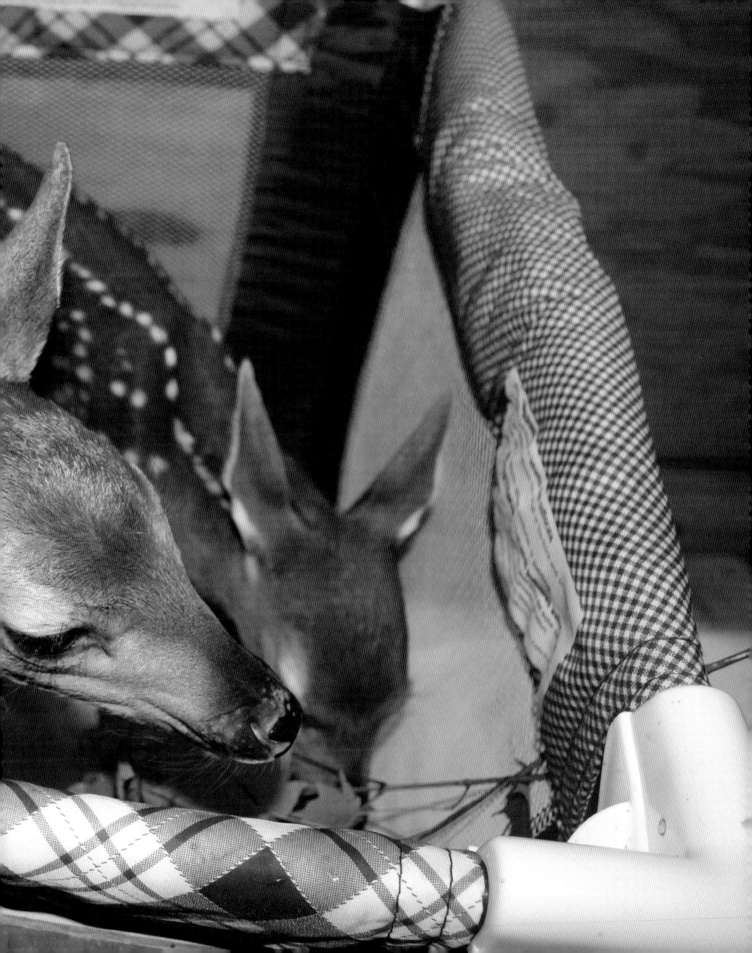

. . . a crate for a bobcat and
even a box for a bunny!

Like firefighters and EMTs, rehabilitators rescue animals that have been injured or trapped. These biologists are rescuing an osprey tangled in fishing line.

Sometimes animals need surgery. A veterinarian operated on this bald eagle. Wildlife rehabilitators are giving him medicine and changing his bandages.

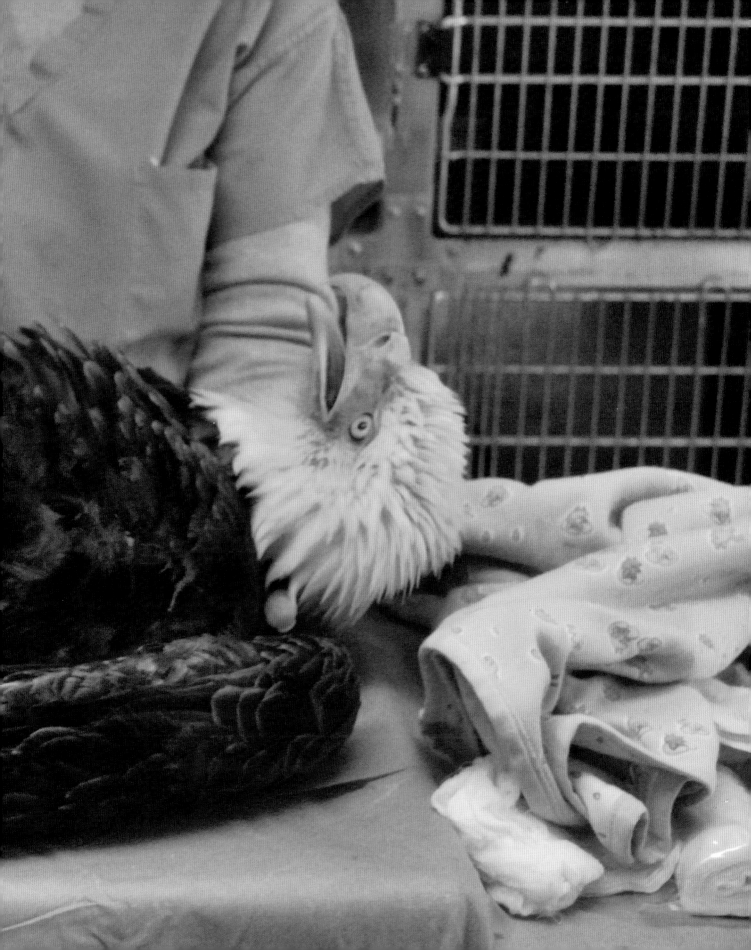

Rehabilitators also mend split shells, cast broken bones, and repair damaged wings.

Rehabilitators are teachers too. They explain the best way to help a wild animal in need and they teach people about the animals.

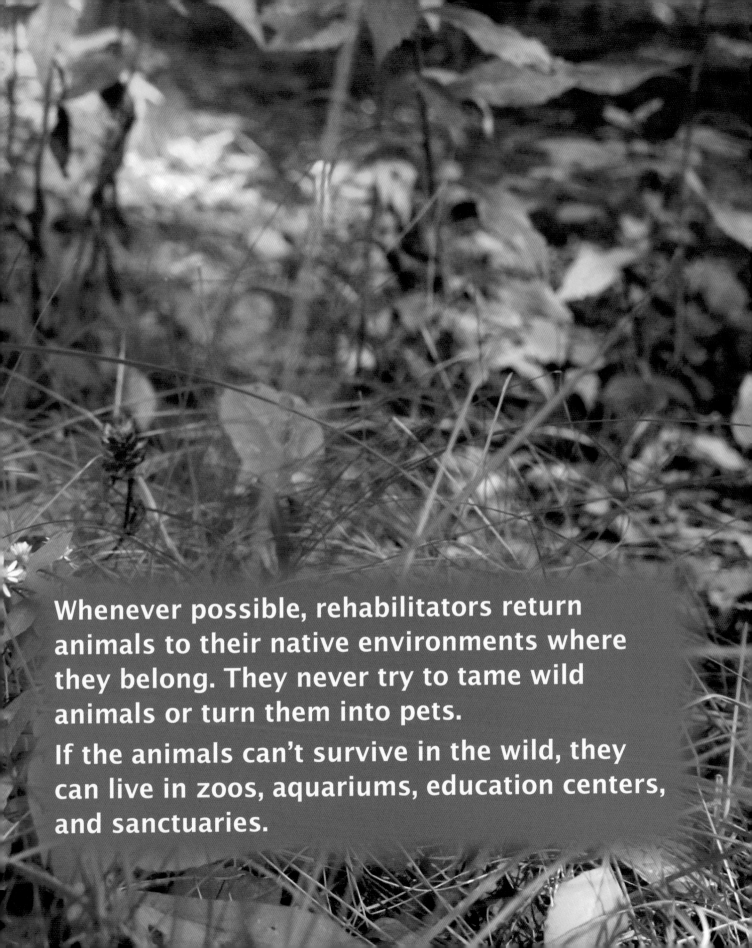

Whenever possible, rehabilitators return animals to their native environments where they belong. They never try to tame wild animals or turn them into pets.

If the animals can't survive in the wild, they can live in zoos, aquariums, education centers, and sanctuaries.

For Creative Minds

Compare and Contrast: Rehabilitators and Veterinarians

Rehabilitators and veterinarians both care for animals.

Veterinarians are doctors who can specialize in animals other than pets, such as wild animals, birds, reptiles, farm animals, and even zoo animals.

Rehabilitators care for injured, ill, and orphaned wild animals with the goal of releasing them back into the wild whenever possible.

Rehabilitators are not doctors. They learn to treat sick and hurt animals by working with veterinarians and master rehabilitators. They also study animal biology and medicine. They must study and pass tests; and, they must have special permits.

Looking at the photos below, can you tell which people are rehabilitators and which are veterinarians?

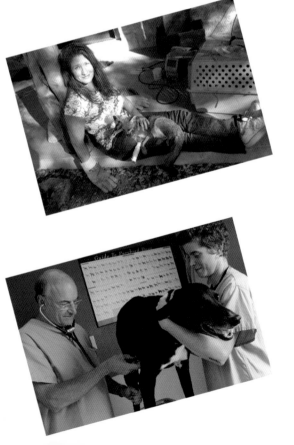

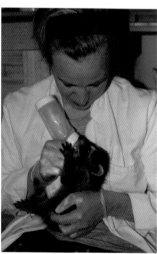

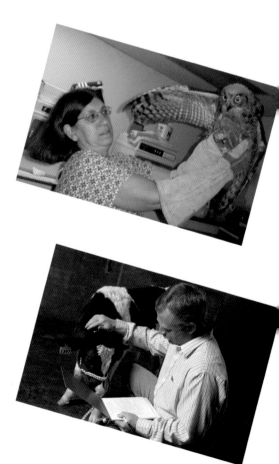

Animal Orphaned or Just Left Alone?

Animal parents raise their babies in different ways. Most reptiles never know their parents and survive on instinct from the minute they hatch. Most birds and mammals, however, do raise their young for a few weeks to a year. Human parents can hire babysitters to care for their young if they have to leave; but wild animal parents don't have critter sitters. Wild animals leave their young alone when they search for food. Sometimes baby animals are found alone and are taken from their nests or homes because humans think the animal has been orphaned; but usually, the mother will soon return. Read the following scenarios to determine if you think the animal has been orphaned or if the parent will return after finding food. Answers, and an explanation of what you should do for the animal, are found at the bottom of the page. If you have any doubt, please try to find the animal helper nearest you.

1. You find a nest of baby bunnies in your yard. The babies are nestled in the mother's fur that she has used to make the nest. You don't see the mother rabbit anywhere.

2. You see a fawn hiding in deep grass near the back of your yard. The mother deer is not around.

3. You find a baby squirrel with very thin fur and eyes that are still closed. You see the nest nearby and hear the mother chattering.

4. You see a fully feathered baby bird (fledgling) sitting quietly on the ground.

5. Near a busy road, you see an animal baby sitting by a mother that appears dead.

Answers: 1. Probably not orphans, keep pets away. Mother rabbits feed their young at dawn and at dusk. 2. Probably waiting for her mother. Leave her alone so that the doe can come back to feed and move her baby. 3. Probably fell, keep pets away and watch to see that the mother gets the baby and puts her back in the nest. 4. Parents are probably watching. Go behind a tree or your house and quietly observe. If the parents are nearby, you'll see them caring for the fledgling. Leave the bird alone and keep pets away. If the bird is a nestling and has fallen out of the nest, you may be able to place him back into that nest if he is unharmed. Then, watch for parents. 5. Orphaned. Call an adult to get the baby right away. Put him in a box and then call a rehabilitator.

Injured Animal True or False

Are these statements true or false?

1. If you pick up a bird to put him back in the nest, the parents will reject him.

2. Most bird parents will look for their missing young for up to four days.

3. It's illegal to keep most wild animals as pets.

4. Wild animals are usually scared of humans and see us as a source of danger and as predators. They become stressed if we pick them up.

5. Predators are attracted to anything that moves differently or makes noises. Wild animals will suffer in silence to avoid attracting predators.

6. Any veterinarian can care for an injured wild animal.

7. An adult turtle crossing the road in the spring is probably trying to find a place to dig a nest to lay her eggs.

8. Turtles stay within the same 5-mile area for their entire lives. If you move a turtle, she will always search for her home.

9. A healthy animal's best chance of survival is to stay with his family in his natural habitat.

10. Wild animals can give humans and pets diseases.

11. You should not try to feed a wild animal or provide a drink.

12. If an animal is bleeding, it's injured.

13. Feathered songbirds (fledglings) often fall when learning to fly. The parents will continue to care for them even though they are on the ground.

Answers: 1) False, the parents will care for their young if returned to the nest or area. 2) True 3) True, Wildlife Rehabilitators need special permits to care for animals. 4) True 5) True 6) False, while veterinarians do know a lot about most animals, wildlife rehabilitators have the permits and the specialized training to care for wild animals. 7) True 8) True 9) True 10) True 11) True 12) True 13) True. If you are not sure the parents are nearby and you are concerned, you may put the bird in a nearby bush or on a tree branch and observe from inside the house for a few hours. If the mother sees you near the nest, she will not return. Keep pets away from the area.

14. If a partially feathered baby bird (nestling) is alert and opening her mouth for food, you can put her back in the nest. If she does not open her mouth for food or appears injured, she needs help.

15. Baby birds less than five days old don't have feathers yet (hatchlings). If they fall from a nest, call a rehabilitator right away.

16. A young rabbit is on his own if the fur is fluffy, the ears stand up, and he is the size of a tennis ball. Unless you see blood or injuries, you should leave him alone.

17. Baby raccoons, skunks, and foxes explore the world around them with their mothers watching nearby—even if you don't see the mothers.

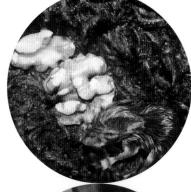

18. Baby groundhogs might wash out of their burrows in heavy rain.

19. Opossums are on their own when they are about the size of a kitten (not including the tail). If you find one smaller than that and she is alone, she probably needs help.

20. Bat babies (called pups) are often found in the summer, having fallen from trees. They look just like the adults but don't fly very well. Young bats that have fallen probably need help. If you find bats in your house, call a rehabilitator for help. Do not ever pick up bats of any size with your bare hands.

21. Even young bears, bobcats, and mountain lions can be very dangerous. Report animal sightings to your local game commission but don't try to handle yourself.

22. Bird parents can pick up their young with their beaks.

23. Baby birds drink milk.

24. A bird hopping around on a branch can't fly.

25. If you need to get an animal to a wildlife rehabilitator, call the rehabilitator for directions on how to pick up, protect, and transport the animal with an adult's help.

As darling as wild animals may seem, they are not pets. To get the best care for an injured or orphaned animal, call a wildlife rehabilitator for advice. To find the animal helper nearest you, visit NWRAwildlife.org or wildliferehabber.org; ask a local veterinarian for a reference; or even call your state Department of Natural Resources, Wildlife Department, or Fish and Game Offices.

Thanks to the following wildlife rehabilitators and photographers for sharing their love of animals with us:

Kathy Woods and Hugh Simmons: Phoenix Wildlife Center, Maryland; www.phoenixwildlife.org

Kim Johnson: Drift Inn Wildlife Sanctuary, Texas; www.thedriftinn.org

Victoria Campbell: Wild Things Sanctuary, New York; www.wildthingssanctuary.org

Miriam Moyer and Mary Birney: White Flicker Wild Bird Rehabilitation Clinic, Pennsylvania; www.whiteflicker.org

Randy Loftus, US Fish and Wildlife Service, Maryland

The American Veterinary Medical Association (AVMA) for use of the veterinarian photos.

Publisher's Cataloging-In-Publication Data
Curtis, Jennifer Keats.
 Animal helpers. Wildlife rehabilitators / by Jennifer Keats Curtis ; with Mary Birney ... [et al.].

 p. : col. ill. ; cm. -- (Animal helpers)

 Summary: The book takes readers "behind the scenes" at four different wildlife rehabilitation centers, where animals are nursed back to health and released back into the wild when possible. Includes "For Creative Minds" educational section.
 Issued also as downloadable ebooks in English and Spanish, as well as a web-based interactive ebook with selectable English or Spanish text.
 ISBN: 978-1-60718-671-7 (hardcover)
 ISBN: 978-1-60718-672-4 (pbk.)

 1. Wildlife rehabilitators--United States--Juvenile literature. 2. Wildlife rehabilitation--United States--Juvenile literature. 3. Wildlife rescue--United States--Juvenile literature. 4. Wildlife rescue--United State. I. Birney, Mary. II. Title. III. Title: Wildlife rehabilitators

SF996.45 .C87 2012
639.9   2012937373

eBook ISBNs
Downloadable English ISBN: 978-1-60718-673-1
Downloadable Spanish ISBN: 978-1-60718-674-8
Interactive Dual Language ISBN: 978-1-60718-675-5

Lexile Level: 890

Manufactured in China, June, 2013
This product conforms to CPSIA 2008
Second Printing

Sylvan Dell Publishing
Mt. Pleasant, SC 29464